'I cried tell me how you live!" And thumped him on the head.'

LEWIS CARROLL
Born 1832, Daresbury, England
Died 1898, Guildford, England

Selected from *Jabberwocky and Other Nonsense:
Collected Poems*, edited by Gillian Beer and
published in Penguin Classics in 2012.

LEWIS CARROLL IN PENGUIN CLASSICS
Alice's Adventures in Wonderland
and *Through the Looking Glass*
The Hunting of the Snark
*Jabberwocky and Other Nonsense:
Collected Poems*

LEWIS CARROLL

O Frabjous Day!

PENGUIN BOOKS

PENGUIN CLASSICS

UK | USA | Canada | Ireland | Australia
India | New Zealand | South Africa

Penguin Classics is part of the Penguin Random House group of companies
whose addresses can be found at global.penguinrandomhouse.com.

Penguin
Random House
UK

This selection first published in Penguin Classics 2016
001

Set in 9.5/13 pt Baskerville 10 Pro
Typeset by Jouve (UK), Milton Keynes
Printed in Great Britain by Clays Ltd, St Ives plc

A CIP catalogue record for this book is available from the British Library

ISBN: 978-0-241-25193-5

www.greenpenguin.co.uk

MIX
Paper from
responsible sources
FSC® C018179

Penguin Random House is committed to a
sustainable future for our business, our readers
and our planet. This book is made from Forest
Stewardship Council® certified paper.

Contents

Brother and Sister

'Sister, sister, go to bed,
Go and rest your weary head,'
Thus the prudent brother said.

'Do you want a battered hide
Or scratches to your face applied?'
Thus the sister calm replied.

'Sister! Do not rouse my wrath,
I'd make you into mutton broth
As easily as kill a moth.'

The sister raised her beaming eye,
And looked on him indignantly,
And sternly answered 'Only try!'

Off to the cook he quickly ran,
'Dear cook, pray lend a frying pan
To me, as quickly as you can.'

'And wherefore should I give it to you?'
'The reason, cook, is plain to view,
I wish to make an Irish stew.'

'What meat is in that stew to go?'
'My sister'll be the contents.' 'Oh!'
'Will you lend the pan, Cook?' 'NO!'

Moral: 'Never stew your sister.'

The Two Brothers

There were two brothers at Twyford school,
    And when they had left the place,
It was, 'Will ye learn Greek and Latin?
    Or will ye run me a race?
Or will ye go up to yonder bridge,
    And there we will angle for dace?'

'I'm too stupid for Greek and for Latin,
    I'm too lazy by half for a race,
So I'll even go up to yonder bridge,
    And there we will angle for dace.'

He has fitted together two joints of his rod,
    And to them he has added another,
And then a great hook he took from his book,
    And ran it right into his brother.

Oh much is the noise that is made among boys
    When playfully pelting a pig,
But a far greater pother was made by his brother
    When flung from the top of the brigg.

The fish hurried up by the dozens,
    All ready and eager to bite,
For the lad that he flung was so tender and young,
    It quite gave them an appetite.

Said he, 'Thus shall he wallop about
　　And the fish take him quite at their ease,
For me to annoy it was ever his joy,
　　Now I'll teach him the meaning of "Tees"!'

The wind to his ear brought a voice,
　　'My brother, you didn't had ought ter!
And what have I done that you think it such fun
　　To indulge in the pleasure of slaughter?

'A good nibble or bite is my chiefest delight,
　　When I'm merely expected to *see*,
But a bite from a fish is not quite what I wish,
　　When I get it performed upon *me*;
And just now here's a swarm of dace at my arm,
　　And a perch has got hold of my knee!

'For water my thirst was not great at the first,
　　And of fish I have had quite sufficien–'
'Oh fear not!' he cried, 'for whatever betide,
　　We are both in the selfsame condition!

'I am sure that our state's very nearly alike
　　(Not considering the question of slaughter),
For I have my perch on the top of the bridge,
　　And you have your perch in the water.

'I stick to my perch and your perch sticks to you,
    We are really extremely alike;
I've a turn-pike up here, and I very much fear
    You may soon have a turn with a pike.'

'Oh, grant but one wish! If I'm took by a fish
    (For your bait is your brother, good man!)
Pull him up if you like, but I hope you will strike
    As gently as ever you can.'

'If the fish be a trout, I'm afraid there's no doubt
    I must strike him like lightning that's greased;
If the fish be a pike, I'll engage not to strike,
    'Till I've waited ten minutes at least.'

'But in those ten minutes to desolate Fate
    Your brother a victim may fall!'
'I'll reduce it to five, so *perhaps* you'll survive,
    But the chance is exceedingly small.'

'Oh hard is your heart for to act such a part;
    Is it iron, or granite, or steel?'
'Why, I really can't say – it is many a day
    Since my heart was accustomed to feel.

''Twas my heart-cherished wish for to slay many fish,
    Each day did my malice grow worse,
For my heart didn't soften with doing it so often,
    But rather, I should say, the reverse.'

'Oh would I were back at Twyford school,
  Learning lessons in fear of the birch!'
'Nay, brother!' he cried, 'for whatever betide,
  You are better off here with your perch!

'I am sure you'll allow you are happier now,
  With nothing to do but to play;
And this single line here, it is perfectly clear,
  Is much better than thirty a day!

'And as to the rod hanging over your head,
  And apparently ready to fall,
That, you know, was the case, when you lived in
   that place,
  So it need not be reckoned at all.

'Do you see that old trout with a turn-up-nose snout?
  (Just to speak on a pleasanter theme,)
Observe, my dear brother, our love for each other –
  He's the one I like best in the stream.

'To-morrow I mean to invite him to dine
  (We shall all of us think it a treat,)
If the day should be fine, I'll just *drop him a line*,
  And we'll settle what time we're to meet.

'He hasn't been into society yet,
  And his manners are not of the best,
So I think it quite fair that it should be *my* care,
  To see that he's properly dressed.'

Many words brought the wind of 'cruel' and 'kind',
    And that 'man suffers more than the brute':
Each several word with patience he heard,
    And answered with wisdom to boot.

'What? prettier swimming in the stream,
    Than lying all snugly and flat?
Do but look at that dish filled with glittering fish,
    Has Nature a picture like that?

'What? a higher delight to be drawn from the sight
    Of fish full of life and of glee?
What a noodle you are! 'tis delightfuller far
    To kill them than let them go free!

'I know there are people who prate by the hour
    Of the beauty of earth, sky, and ocean;
Of the birds as they fly, of the fish darting by,
    Rejoicing in Life and in Motion.

'As to any delight to be got from the sight,
    It is all very well for a flat,
But *I* think it all gammon, for hooking a salmon
    Is better than twenty of that!

'They say that a man of a right-thinking mind
    Will *love* the dumb creatures he sees –
What's the use of his mind, if he's never inclined
    To pull a fish out of the Tees?

'Take my friends and my home – as an outcast I'll roam:
    Take the money I have in the Bank –
It is just what I wish, but deprive me of *fish*,
    And my life would indeed be a blank!'

Forth from the house his sister came,
    Her brothers for to see,
But when she saw that sight of awe,
    The tear stood in her ee.

'Oh what bait's that upon your hook,
    My brother, tell to me?'
'It is but the fantailed pigeon,
    He would not sing for me.'

'Whoe'er would expect a pigeon to sing,
    A simpleton he must be!
But a pigeon-cote is a different thing
    To the coat that there I see!

'Oh what bait's that upon your hook,
    My brother, tell to me?'
'It is but the black-capped bantam,
    He would not dance for me.'

'And a pretty dance you are leading him now!'
    In anger answered she,
'But a bantam's cap is a different thing
    To the cap that there I see!

'Oh what bait's that upon your hook
    Dear brother, tell to me?'
'It is my younger brother,' he cried,
    'Oh woe and dole is me!

'I's mighty wicked, that I is!
    Or how could such things be?
Farewell, farewell, sweet sister,
    I'm going o'er the sea.'

'And when will you come back again,
    My brother, tell to me?'
'When chub is good for human food,
    And that will never be!'

She turned herself right round about,
    And her heart brake into three,
Said, 'One of the two will be wet through and
      through,
    And t'other'll be late for his tea!'

Croft. 1853

The Dear Gazelle

THE DEAR GAZELLE
ARRANGED WITH VARIATIONS

espressivo
" I never loved a dear gazelle,"
Nor aught beside that cost me much ;
High prices profit those who sell,
But why should *I* be fond of such ?

p.p   *cres :*———
" To glad me with his soft black eyes,"
My infant son, from Tooting School,
Thrashed by his bigger playmate, flies ;
And serve him right, the little fool !
con spirito

A Tempo
" But when he came to know me well,"
He kicked me out, her testy sire ;
And when I stained my hair, that Bell
Might note the change, and thus admire

dim :   *cadenza*   *D.C.*
" And love me, it was sure to die "
A muddy green, or staring blue,
While one might trace, with half an eye,
The still triumphant carrot through.
con dolore

CH: CH: 1855.

[‘How doth the little crocodile’]

How doth the little crocodile
    Improve his shining tail,
And pour the waters of the Nile
    On every golden scale!

How cheerfully he seems to grin,
    How neatly spreads his claws,
And welcomes little fishes in,
    With gently smiling jaws!

[' "You are old, Father William," the young man said']

'You are old, Father William,' the young man said,
    'And your hair has become very white;
And yet you incessantly stand on your head –
    Do you think, at your age, it is right?'

'In my youth,' Father William replied to his son,
    'I feared it might injure the brain;
But, now that I'm perfectly sure I have none,
    Why, I do it again and again.'

'You are old,' said the youth, 'as I mentioned before,
    And have grown most uncommonly fat;
Yet you turned a back-somersault in at the door –
    Pray, what is the reason for that?'

'In my youth,' said the sage, as he shook his grey locks,
    'I kept all my limbs very supple
By the use of this ointment – one shilling the box –
    Allow me to sell you a couple?'

'You are old,' said the youth, 'and your jaws are too weak
    For anything tougher than suet;
Yet you finished the goose, with the bones and the beak –
    Pray, how did you manage to do it?'

'In my youth,' said his father, 'I took to the law,
  And argued each case with my wife;
And the muscular strength, which it gave to my jaw
  Has lasted the rest of my life.'

'You are old,' said the youth, 'one would hardly suppose
  That your eye was as steady as ever;
Yet you balanced an eel on the end of your nose –
  What made you so awfully clever?'

'I have answered three questions, and that is enough,'
  Said his father. 'Don't give yourself airs!
Do you think I can listen all day to such stuff?
  Be off, or I'll kick you down-stairs!'

[The Mock Turtle's Song: I]

'Will you walk a little faster?' said a whiting to a snail,
'There's a porpoise close behind us, and he's treading
      on my tail.
See how eagerly the lobsters and the turtles all advance!
They are waiting on the shingle – will you come and
      join the dance?
    Will you, won't you, will you, won't you, will you
      join the dance?
    Will you, won't you, will you, won't you, won't
      you join the dance?

'You can really have no notion how delightful it will be
When they take us up and throw us, with the lobsters,
      out to sea!'
But the snail replied 'Too far, too far!', and gave a look
      askance –
Said he thanked the whiting kindly, but he would not
      join the dance.
    Would not, could not, would not, could not,
      would not join the dance.
    Would not, could not, would not, could not,
      could not join the dance.

'What matters it how far we go?' his scaly friend replied.
'There is another shore, you know, upon the other side.
The further off from England the nearer is to France –
Then turn not pale, beloved snail, but come and join
     the dance.
     Will you, won't you, will you, won't you, will you
       join the dance?
     Will you, won't you, will you, won't you, won't
       you join the dance?'

[' 'Tis the voice of the Lobster: I heard him declare']

'Tis the voice of the Lobster: I heard him declare
'You have baked me too brown, I must sugar my hair.'
As a duck with his eyelids, so he with his nose
Trims his belt and his buttons, and turns out his toes.

When the sands are all dry, he is gay as a lark,
And will talk in contemptuous tones of the Shark:
But, when the tide rises and sharks are around,
His voice has a timid and tremulous sound.

Jabberwocky

Jabberwocky

'Twas brillig, and the slithy toves
Did gyre and gimble in the wabe:
All mimsy were the borogoves,
And the mome raths outgrabe.

'Twas brillig, and the slithy toves
    Did gyre and gimble in the wabe:
All mimsy were the borogoves,
    And the mome raths outgrabe.

'Beware the Jabberwock, my son!
    The jaws that bite, the claws that catch!
Beware the Jubjub bird, and shun
    The frumious Bandersnatch!'

He took his vorpal sword in hand:
    Long time the manxome foe he sought –
So rested he by the Tumtum tree,
    And stood awhile in thought.

And, as in uffish thought he stood,
    The Jabberwock, with eyes of flame,
Came whiffling through the tulgey wood,
    And burbled as it came!

One, two! One, two! And through and through
     The vorpal blade went snicker-snack!
He left it dead, and with its head
     He went galumphing back.

'And, hast thou slain the Jabberwock?
     Come to my arms, my beamish boy!
O frabjous day! Callooh! Callay!'
     He chortled in his joy.

'Twas brillig, and the slithy toves
     Did gyre and gimble in the wabe:
All mimsy were the borogoves,
     And the mome raths outgrabe.

The Walrus and the Carpenter

The sun was shining on the sea,
　　Shining with all his might:
He did his very best to make
　　The billows smooth and bright –
And this was odd, because it was
　　The middle of the night.

The moon was shining sulkily,
　　Because she thought the sun
Had got no business to be there
　　After the day was done –
'It's very rude of him,' she said,
　　'To come and spoil the fun.'

The sea was wet as wet could be,
　　The sands were dry as dry.
You could not see a cloud, because
　　No cloud was in the sky:
No birds were flying overhead –
　　There were no birds to fly.

The Walrus and the Carpenter
　　Were walking close at hand.
They wept like anything to see
　　Such quantities of sand:
'If this were only cleared away,'
　　They said, 'it *would* be grand!'

'If seven maids with seven mops
  Swept it for half a year,
Do you suppose,' the Walrus said,
  'That they could get it clear?'
'I doubt it,' said the Carpenter,
  And shed a bitter tear.

'O Oysters, come and walk with us!'
  The Walrus did beseech.
'A pleasant walk, a pleasant talk,
  Along the briny beach:
We cannot do with more than four,
  To give a hand to each.'

The eldest Oyster looked at him,
  But never a word he said:
The eldest Oyster winked his eye,
  And shook his heavy head –
Meaning to say he did not choose
  To leave the oyster-bed.

But four young Oysters hurried up,
  All eager for the treat:
Their coats were brushed, their faces washed,
  Their shoes were clean and neat –
And this was odd, because, you know,
  They hadn't any feet.

Four other Oysters followed them,
    And yet another four;
And thick and fast they came at last,
    And more, and more, and more –
All hopping through the frothy waves,
    And scrambling to the shore.

The Walrus and the Carpenter
    Walked on a mile or so,
And then they rested on a rock
    Conveniently low:
And all the little Oysters stood
    And waited in a row.

'The time has come,' the Walrus said,
    'To talk of many things:
Of shoes – and ships – and sealing-wax –
    Of cabbages – and kings –
And why the sea is boiling hot –
    And whether pigs have wings.'

'But wait a bit,' the Oysters cried,
    'Before we have our chat:
For some of us are out of breath,
    And all of us are fat!'
'No hurry!' said the Carpenter.
    They thanked him much for that.

'A loaf of bread,' the Walrus said,
    'Is what we chiefly need:
Pepper and vinegar besides
    Are very good indeed –
Now if you're ready, Oysters dear,
    We can begin to feed.'

'But not on us!' the Oysters cried,
    Turning a little blue.
'After such kindness, that would be
    A dismal thing to do!'
'The night is fine,' the Walrus said.
    'Do you admire the view?

'It was so kind of you to come!
    And you are very nice!'
The Carpenter said nothing but
    'Cut us another slice,
I wish you were not quite so deaf –
    I've had to ask you twice!'

'It seems a shame,' the Walrus said,
    'To play them such a trick,
After we've brought them out so far,
    And made them trot so quick!'
The Carpenter said nothing but
    'The butter's spread too thick!'

'I weep for you,' the Walrus said:
    'I deeply sympathise.'
With sobs and tears he sorted out
    Those of the largest size,
Holding his pocket-handkerchief
    Before his streaming eyes.

'O Oysters,' said the Carpenter,
    'You've had a pleasant run!
Shall we be trotting home again?'
    But answer came there none –
And this was scarcely odd, because
    They'd eaten every one.

[The White Knight's Song]

I'll tell thee everything I can:
    There's little to relate.
I saw an aged, aged man,
    A-sitting on a gate.
'Who are you, aged man?' I said.
    'And how is it you live?'
And his answer trickled through my head,
    Like water through a sieve.

He said, 'I look for butterflies
    That sleep among the wheat;
I make them into mutton-pies,
    And sell them in the street.
I sell them unto men,' he said,
    'Who sail on stormy seas;
And that's the way I get my bread –
    A trifle, if you please.'

But I was thinking of a plan
    To dye one's whiskers green,
And always use so large a fan
    That they could not be seen.
So, having no reply to give
    To what the old man said,
I cried, 'Come, tell me how you live!'
    And thumped him on the head.

His accents mild took up the tale:
    He said, 'I go my ways,
And when I find a mountain-rill,
    I set it in a blaze;
And thence they make a stuff they call
    Rowland's Macassar-Oil –
Yet twopence-halfpenny is all
    They give me for my toil.'

But I was thinking of a way
    To feed oneself on batter,
And so go on from day to day
    Getting a little fatter.
I shook him well from side to side,
    Until his face was blue,
'Come, tell me how you live,' I cried,
    'And what it is you do!'

He said, 'I hunt for haddocks' eyes
    Among the heather bright,
And work them into waistcoat-buttons
    In the silent night.
And these I do not sell for gold
    Or coin of silvery shine,
But for a copper halfpenny,
    And that will purchase nine.

'I sometimes dig for buttered rolls,
    Or set limed twigs for crabs;
I sometimes search the grassy knolls
    For wheels of hansom-cabs.
And that's the way' (he gave a wink)
    'By which I get my wealth –
And very gladly will I drink
    Your Honour's noble health.'

I heard him then, for I had just
    Completed my design
To keep the Menai bridge from rust
    By boiling it in wine.
I thanked him much for telling me
    The way he got his wealth,
But chiefly for his wish that he
    Might drink my noble health.

And now, if e'er by chance I put
    My fingers into glue,
Or madly squeeze a right-hand foot
    Into a left-hand shoe,
Or if I drop upon my toe
    A very heavy weight,
I weep, for it reminds me so
Of that old man I used to know –
Whose look was mild, whose speech was slow,
Whose hair was whiter than the snow,

Whose face was very like a crow,
With eyes, like cinders, all aglow,
Who seemed distracted with his woe,
Who rocked his body to and fro,
And muttered mumblingly and low,
As if his mouth were full of dough,
Who snorted like a buffalo –
That summer evening long ago,
    A-sitting on a gate.

[The Gardener's Song]

He thought he saw an Elephant
    That practised on a fife:
He looked again, and found it was
    A letter from his wife.
'At length I realise,' he said,
    'The bitterness of Life.'

He thought he saw a Buffalo
    Upon the chimney-piece:
He looked again, and found it was
    His Sister's Husband's Niece.
'Unless you leave this house,' he said,
    'I'll send for the Police!'

He thought he saw a Rattlesnake
    That questioned him in Greek:
He looked again, and found it was
    The Middle of Next Week.
'The one thing I regret,' he said,
    'Is that it cannot speak!'

He thought he saw a Banker's Clerk
    Descending from the bus:
He looked again, and found it was
    A Hippopotamus.

'If this should stay to dine,' he said,
    'There won't be much for us!'

He thought he saw a Kangaroo
    That worked a coffee-mill:
He looked again, and found it was
    A Vegetable-Pill.
'Were I to swallow this,' he said,
    'I should be very ill!'

He thought he saw a Coach-and-Four
    That stood beside his bed:
He looked again, and found it was
    A Bear without a Head.
'Poor thing,' he said, 'poor silly thing!
    It's waiting to be fed!'

He thought he saw an Albatross
    That fluttered round the lamp:
He looked again, and found it was
    A Penny-Postage-Stamp.
'You'd best be getting home,' he said:
    'The nights are very damp!'

He thought he saw a Garden-Door
    That opened with a key:
He looked again, and found it was
    A Double Rule of Three.
'And all its mystery,' he said,
    'Is clear as day to me!'

He thought he saw an Argument
      That proved he was the Pope:
He looked again, and found it was
      A Bar of Mottled Soap.
'A fact so dread,' he faintly said,
      'Extinguishes all hope!'

from The Hunting of the Snark

'Just the place for a Snark!' the Bellman cried,
   As he landed his crew with care;
Supporting each man on the top of the tide
   By a finger entwined in his hair.

'Just the place for a Snark! I have said it twice:
   That alone should encourage the crew.
Just the place for a Snark! I have said it thrice:
   What I tell you three times is true.'

The crew was complete: it included a Boots –
   A maker of Bonnets and Hoods –
A Barrister, brought to arrange their disputes –
   And a Broker, to value their goods.

A Billiard-marker, whose skill was immense,
   Might perhaps have won more than his share –
But a Banker, engaged at enormous expense,
   Had the whole of their cash in his care.

There was also a Beaver, that paced on the deck,
   Or would sit making lace in the bow:
And had often (the Bellman said) saved them from wreck
   Though none of the sailors knew how.

There was one who was famed for the number of things
    He forgot when he entered the ship:
His umbrella, his watch, all his jewels and rings,
    And the clothes he had bought for the trip.

He had forty-two boxes, all carefully packed,
    With his name painted clearly on each:
But, since he omitted to mention the fact,
    They were all left behind on the beach.

The loss of his clothes hardly mattered, because
    He had seven coats on when he came,
With three pairs of boots – but the worst of it was,
    He had wholly forgotten his name.

He would answer to 'Hi!' or to any loud cry,
    Such as 'Fry me!' or 'Fritter my wig!'
To 'What-you-may-call-um!' or 'What-was-his-name!'
    But especially 'Thing-um-a-jig!'

While, for those who preferred a more forcible word,
    He had different names from these:
His intimate friends called him 'Candle-ends,'
    And his enemies 'Toasted-cheese.'

'His form is ungainly – his intellect small –'
    (So the Bellman would often remark) –
'But his courage is perfect! And that, after all,
    Is the thing that one needs with a Snark.'

He would joke with hyaenas, returning their stare
    With an impudent wag of the head:
And he once went a walk, paw-in-paw, with a bear,
    'Just to keep up its spirits,' he said.

He came as a Baker: but owned, when too late –
    And it drove the poor Bellman half-mad –
He could only bake Bridecake – for which, I may state,
    No materials were to be had.

The last of the crew needs especial remark,
    Though he looked an incredible dunce:
He had just one idea – but, that one being 'Snark,'
    The good Bellman engaged him at once.

He came as a Butcher: but gravely declared,
    When the ship had been sailing a week,
He could only kill Beavers. The Bellman looked scared,
    And was almost too frightened to speak:

But at length he explained, in a tremulous tone,
    There was only one Beaver on board;
And that was a tame one he had of his own,
    Whose death would be deeply deplored.

The Beaver, who happened to hear the remark,
    Protested, with tears in its eyes,
That not even the rapture of hunting the Snark
    Could atone for that dismal surprise!

It strongly advised that the Butcher should be
   Conveyed in a separate ship:
But the Bellman declared that would never agree
   With the plans he had made for the trip:

Navigation was always a difficult art,
   Though with only one ship and one bell:
And he feared he must really decline, for his part,
   Undertaking another as well.

The Beaver's best course was, no doubt, to procure
   A second-hand dagger-proof coat –
So the Baker advised it – and next, to insure
   Its life in some Office of note:

This the Banker suggested, and offered for hire
   (On moderate terms), or for sale,
Two excellent Policies, one Against Fire,
   And one Against Damage From Hail.

Yet still, ever after that sorrowful day,
   Whenever the Butcher was by,
The Beaver kept looking the opposite way,
   And appeared unaccountably shy.

from The Hunting of the Snark

FIT THE SECOND
THE BELLMAN'S SPEECH

The Bellman himself they all praised to the skies –
    Such a carriage, such ease and such grace!
Such solemnity, too! One could see he was wise,
    The moment one looked in his face!

He had bought a large map representing the sea,
    Without the least vestige of land:
And the crew were much pleased when they found it to be
    A map they could all understand.

'What's the good of Mercator's North Poles and Equators,
    Tropics, Zones, and Meridian Lines?'
So the Bellman would cry: and the crew would reply
    'They are merely conventional signs!

'Other maps are such shapes, with their islands and capes!
    But we've got our brave Captain to thank'
(So the crew would protest) 'that he's bought *us* the best –
    A perfect and absolute blank!'

This was charming, no doubt: but they shortly found out
    That the Captain they trusted so well
Had only one notion for crossing the ocean,
    And that was to tingle his bell.

He was thoughtful and grave – but the orders he gave
   Were enough to bewilder a crew.
When he cried 'Steer to starboard, but keep her head
    larboard!'
   What on earth was the helmsman to do?

Then the bowsprit got mixed with the rudder sometimes:
   A thing, as the Bellman remarked,
That frequently happens in tropical climes,
   When a vessel is, so to speak, 'snarked.'

But the principal failing occurred in the sailing,
   And the Bellman, perplexed and distressed,
Said he *had* hoped, at least, when the wind blew due East,
   That the ship would *not* travel due West!

But the danger was past – they had landed at last,
   With their boxes, portmanteaus, and bags:
Yet at first sight the crew were not pleased with the view
   Which consisted of chasms and crags.

The Bellman perceived that their spirits were low,
   And repeated in musical tone
Some jokes he had kept for a season of woe –
   But the crew would do nothing but groan.

He served out some grog with a liberal hand,
   And bade them sit down on the beach:

And they could not but own that their Captain looked
    grand,
  As he stood and delivered his speech.

'Friends, Romans, and countrymen, lend me your ears!'
  (They were all of them fond of quotations:
So they drank to his health, and they gave him three
    cheers,
  While he served out additional rations).

'We have sailed many months, we have sailed many weeks,
  (Four weeks to the month you may mark),
But never as yet ('tis your Captain who speaks)
  Have we caught the least glimpse of a Snark!

'We have sailed many weeks, we have sailed many days,
  (Seven days to the week I allow),
But a Snark, on the which we might lovingly gaze,
  We have never beheld till now!

'Come, listen, my men, while I tell you again
  The five unmistakable marks
By which you may know, wheresoever you go,
  The warranted genuine Snarks.

'Let us take them in order. The first is the taste,
  Which is meagre and hollow, but crisp:
Like a coat that is rather too tight in the waist,
  With a flavour of Will-o'-the-Wisp.

'Its habit of getting up late you'll agree
    That it carries too far, when I say
That it frequently breakfasts at five-o'clock tea,
    And dines on the following day.

'The third is its slowness in taking a jest.
    Should you happen to venture on one,
It will sigh like a thing that is deeply distressed:
    And it always looks grave at a pun.

'The fourth is its fondness for bathing-machines,
    Which it constantly carries about,
And believes that they add to the beauty of scenes –
    A sentiment open to doubt.

'The fifth is ambition. It next will be right
    To describe each particular batch:
Distinguishing those that have feathers, and bite,
    And those that have whiskers, and scratch.

'For, although common Snarks do no manner of harm,
    Yet, I feel it my duty to say,
Some are Boojums –' The Bellman broke off in alarm,
    For the Baker had fainted away.

FIT THE THIRD
THE BAKER'S TALE

They roused him with muffins – they roused him with ice –
  They roused him with mustard and cress –
They roused him with jam and judicious advice –
  They set him conundrums to guess.

When at length he sat up and was able to speak,
  His sad story he offered to tell;
And the Bellman cried 'Silence! Not even a shriek!'
  And excitedly tingled his bell.

There was silence supreme! Not a shriek, not a scream,
  Scarcely even a howl or a groan,
As the man they called 'Ho!' told his story of woe
  In an antediluvian tone.

'My father and mother were honest, though poor –'
  'Skip all that!' cried the Bellman in haste.
'If it once becomes dark, there's no chance of a Snark –
  We have hardly a minute to waste!'

'I skip forty years,' said the Baker in tears,
  'And proceed without further remark
To the day when you took me aboard of your ship
  To help you in hunting the Snark.

'A dear uncle of mine (after whom I was named)
    Remarked, when I bade him farewell –'
'Oh, skip your dear uncle!' the Bellman exclaimed,
    As he angrily tingled his bell.

'He remarked to me then,' said that mildest of men,
    ' "If your Snark be a Snark, that is right:
Fetch it home by all means – you may serve it with greens
    And it's handy for striking a light.

' "You may seek it with thimbles – and seek it with care –
    You may hunt it with forks and hope;
You may threaten its life with a railway-share;
    You may charm it with smiles and soap –" '

('That's exactly the method,' the Bellman bold
    In a hasty parenthesis cried,
'That's exactly the way I have always been told
    That the capture of Snarks should be tried!')

' "But oh, beamish nephew, beware of the day,
    If your Snark be a Boojum! For then
You will softly and suddenly vanish away,
    And never be met with again!"

'It is this, it is this that oppresses my soul,
    When I think of my uncle's last words:
And my heart is like nothing so much as a bowl
    Brimming over with quivering curds!

'It is this, it is this –' 'We have had that before!'
  The Bellman indignantly said.
And the Baker replied 'Let me say it once more.
  It is this, it is this that I dread!

'I engage with the Snark – every night after dark –
  In a dreamy delirious fight:
I serve it with greens in those shadowy scenes,
  And I use it for striking a light:

'But if ever I meet with a Boojum, that day,
  In a moment (of this I am sure),
I shall softly and suddenly vanish away –
  And the notion I cannot endure!'

FIT THE FOURTH
THE HUNTING

The Bellman looked uffish, and wrinkled his brow.
  'If only you'd spoken before!
It's excessively awkward to mention it now,
  With the Snark, so to speak, at the door!

'We should all of us grieve, as you well may believe,
  If you never were met with again –
But surely, my man, when the voyage began,
  You might have suggested it then?

'It's excessively awkward to mention it now –
    As I think I've already remarked.'
And the man they called 'Hi!' replied, with a sigh,
    'I informed you the day we embarked.

'You may charge me with murder – or want of sense –
    (We are all of us weak at times):
But the slightest approach to a false pretence
    Was never among my crimes!

'I said it in Hebrew – I said it in Dutch –
    I said it in German and Greek:
But I wholly forgot (and it vexes me much)
    That English is what you speak!'

''Tis a pitiful tale,' said the Bellman, whose face
    Had grown longer at every word:
'But, now that you've stated the whole of your case,
    More debate would be simply absurd.

'The rest of my speech' (he explained to his men)
    'You shall hear when I've leisure to speak it.
But the Snark is at hand, let me tell you again!
    'Tis your glorious duty to seek it!

'To seek it with thimbles, to seek it with care;
    To pursue it with forks and hope;
To threaten its life with a railway-share;
    To charm it with smiles and soap!

'For the Snark's a peculiar creature, that won't
    Be caught in a commonplace way.
Do all that you know, and try all that you don't:
    Not a chance must be wasted to-day!

'For England expects – I forbear to proceed:
    'Tis a maxim tremendous, but trite:
And you'd best be unpacking the things that you need
    To rig yourselves out for the fight.'

Then the Banker endorsed a blank cheque (which
       he crossed),
    And changed his loose silver for notes:
The Baker with care combed his whiskers and hair,
    And shook the dust out of his coats:

The Boots and the Broker were sharpening a spade –
    Each working the grindstone in turn:
But the Beaver went on making lace, and displayed
    No interest in the concern:

Though the Barrister tried to appeal to its pride,
    And vainly proceeded to cite
A number of cases, in which making laces
    Had been proved an infringement of right.

The maker of Bonnets ferociously planned
    A novel arrangement of bows:
While the Billiard-marker with quivering hand
    Was chalking the tip of his nose.

But the Butcher turned nervous, and dressed himself fine,
    With yellow kid gloves and a ruff –
Said he felt it exactly like going to dine,
    Which the Bellman declared was all 'stuff.'

'Introduce me, now there's a good fellow,' he said,
    'If we happen to meet it together!'
And the Bellman, sagaciously nodding his head,
    Said 'That must depend on the weather.'

The Beaver went simply galumphing about,
    At seeing the Butcher so shy:
And even the Baker, though stupid and stout,
    Made an effort to wink with one eye.

'Be a man!' said the Bellman in wrath, as he heard
    The Butcher beginning to sob.
'Should we meet with a Jubjub, that desperate bird,
    We shall need all our strength for the job!'

FIT THE FIFTH
THE BEAVER'S LESSON

They sought it with thimbles, they sought it with care;
    They pursued it with forks and hope;
They threatened its life with a railway-share;
    They charmed it with smiles and soap.

Then the Butcher contrived an ingenious plan
    For making a separate sally;
And had fixed on a spot unfrequented by man,
    A dismal and desolate valley.

But the very same plan to the Beaver occurred:
    It had chosen the very same place:
Yet neither betrayed, by a sign or a word,
    The disgust that appeared in his face.

Each thought he was thinking of nothing but 'Snark'
    And the glorious work of the day;
And each tried to pretend that he did not remark
    That the other was going that way.

But the valley grew narrow and narrower still,
    And the evening got darker and colder,
Till (merely from nervousness, not from goodwill)
    They marched along shoulder to shoulder.

Then a scream, shrill and high, rent the shuddering sky,
    And they knew that some danger was near:
The Beaver turned pale to the tip of its tail,
    And even the Butcher felt queer.

He thought of his childhood, left far far behind –
    That blissful and innocent state –
The sound so exactly recalled to his mind
    A pencil that squeaks on a slate!

' 'Tis the voice of the Jubjub!' he suddenly cried.
   (This man, that they used to call 'Dunce.')
'As the Bellman would tell you,' he added with pride,
   'I have uttered that sentiment once.

' 'Tis the note of the Jubjub! Keep count, I entreat.
   You will find I have told it you twice.
'Tis the song of the Jubjub! The proof is complete.
   If only I've stated it thrice.'

The Beaver had counted with scrupulous care,
   Attending to every word:
But it fairly lost heart, and outgrabe in despair,
   When the third repetition occurred.

It felt that, in spite of all possible pains,
   It had somehow contrived to lose count,
And the only thing now was to rack its poor brains
   By reckoning up the amount.

'Two added to one – if that could but be done,'
   It said, 'with one's fingers and thumbs!'
Recollecting with tears how, in earlier years,
   It had taken no pains with its sums.

'The thing can be done,' said the Butcher, 'I think.
   The thing must be done, I am sure.
The thing shall be done! Bring me paper and ink,
   The best there is time to procure.'

The Beaver brought paper, portfolio, pens,
    And ink in unfailing supplies:
While strange creepy creatures came out of their dens,
    And watched them with wondering eyes.

So engrossed was the Butcher, he heeded them not,
    As he wrote with a pen in each hand,
And explained all the while in a popular style
    Which the Beaver could well understand.

'Taking Three as the subject to reason about –
    A convenient number to state –
We add Seven, and Ten, and then multiply out
    By One Thousand diminished by Eight.

'The result we proceed to divide, as you see,
    By Nine Hundred and Ninety and Two:
Then subtract Seventeen, and the answer must be
    Exactly and perfectly true.

'The method employed I would gladly explain,
    While I have it so clear in my head,
If I had but the time and you had but the brain –
    But much yet remains to be said.

'In one moment I've seen what has hitherto been
    Enveloped in absolute mystery,
And without extra charge I will give you at large
    A Lesson in Natural History.'

In his genial way he proceeded to say
    (Forgetting all laws of propriety,
And that giving instruction, without introduction,
    Would have caused quite a thrill in Society),

'As to temper the Jubjub's a desperate bird,
    Since it lives in perpetual passion:
Its taste in costume is entirely absurd –
    It is ages ahead of the fashion:

'But it knows any friend it has met once before:
    It never will look at a bribe:
And in charity-meetings it stands at the door,
    And collects – though it does not subscribe.

'Its flavour when cooked is more exquisite far
    Than mutton, or oysters, or eggs:
(Some think it keeps best in an ivory jar,
    And some, in mahogany kegs:)

'You boil it in sawdust: you salt it in glue:
    You condense it with locusts and tape:
Still keeping one principal object in view –
    To preserve its symmetrical shape.'

The Butcher would gladly have talked till next day,
    But he felt that the lesson must end,
And he wept with delight in attempting to say
    He considered the Beaver his friend:

While the Beaver confessed, with affectionate looks
    More eloquent even than tears,
It had learned in ten minutes far more than all books
    Would have taught it in seventy years.

They returned hand-in-hand, and the Bellman, unmanned
    (For a moment) with noble emotion,
Said 'This amply repays all the wearisome days
    We have spent on the billowy ocean!'

Such friends, as the Beaver and Butcher became,
    Have seldom if ever been known;
In winter or summer, 'twas always the same –
    You could never meet either alone.

And when quarrels arose – as one frequently finds
    Quarrels will, spite of every endeavour –
The song of the Jubjub recurred to their minds,
    And cemented their friendship for ever!

FIT THE SEVENTH
THE BANKER'S FATE

They sought it with thimbles, they sought it with care;
    They pursued it with forks and hope;
They threatened its life with a railway-share;
    They charmed it with smiles and soap.

And the Banker, inspired with a courage so new
   It was matter for general remark,
Rushed madly ahead and was lost to their view
   In his zeal to discover the Snark.

But while he was seeking with thimbles and care,
   A Bandersnatch swiftly drew nigh
And grabbed at the Banker, who shrieked in despair,
   For he knew it was useless to fly.

He offered large discount – he offered a cheque
   (Drawn 'to bearer') for seven-pounds-ten:
But the Bandersnatch merely extended its neck
   And grabbed at the Banker again.

Without rest or pause – while those frumious jaws
   Went savagely snapping around –
He skipped and he hopped, and he floundered and
     flopped,
   Till fainting he fell to the ground.

The Bandersnatch fled as the others appeared
   Led on by that fear-stricken yell:
And the Bellman remarked 'It is just as I feared!'
   And solemnly tolled on his bell.

He was black in the face, and they scarcely could trace
    The least likeness to what he had been:
While so great was his fright that his waistcoat turned white –
    A wonderful thing to be seen!

To the horror of all who were present that day,
    He uprose in full evening dress,
And with senseless grimaces endeavoured to say
    What his tongue could no longer express.

Down he sank in a chair – ran his hands through his hair –
    And chanted in mimsiest tones
Words whose utter inanity proved his insanity,
    While he rattled a couple of bones.

'Leave him here to his fate – it is getting so late!'
    The Bellman exclaimed in a fright.
'We have lost half the day. Any further delay,
    And we shan't catch a Snark before night!'

FIT THE EIGHTH
THE VANISHING

They sought it with thimbles, they sought it with care;
    They pursued it with forks and hope;
They threatened its life with a railway-share;
    They charmed it with smiles and soap.

They shuddered to think that the chase might fail,
    And the Beaver, excited at last,
Went bounding along on the tip of its tail,
    For the daylight was nearly past.

'There is Thingumbob shouting!' the Bellman said,
    'He is shouting like mad, only hark!
He is waving his hands, he is wagging his head,
    He has certainly found a Snark!'

They gazed in delight, while the Butcher exclaimed
    'He was always a desperate wag!'
They beheld him – their Baker – their hero unnamed –
    On the top of a neighbouring crag,

Erect and sublime, for one moment of time,
    In the next, that wild figure they saw
(As if stung by a spasm) plunge into a chasm,
    While they waited and listened in awe.

'It's a Snark!' was the sound that first came to their ears,
    And seemed almost too good to be true.
Then followed a torrent of laughter and cheers:
    Then the ominous words 'It's a Boo –'

Then, silence. Some fancied they heard in the air
    A weary and wandering sigh
That sounded like '–jum!' but the others declare
    It was only a breeze that went by.

They hunted till darkness came on, but they found
    Not a button, or feather, or mark,
By which they could tell that they stood on the ground
    Where the Baker had met with the Snark.

In the midst of the word he was trying to say,
    In the midst of his laughter and glee,
He had softly and suddenly vanished away –
    For the Snark *was* a Boojum, you see.